Count with Me

counting with
ALIENS

by William Anthony

Gareth Stevens
PUBLISHING

T0004834

Please visit our website, www.garethstevens.com.
For a free color catalog of all our high-quality books,
call toll free 1-800-542-2595 or fax 1-877-542-2596.

Cataloging-in-Publication Data

Names: Anthony, William, author. | Li, Amy, illustrator.
Title: Counting with aliens / by William Anthony, illustrated by Amy Li.
Description: New York : Gareth Stevens, 2023. | Series: Count with me
Identifiers: ISBN 9781538281703 (pbk.) | ISBN 9781538281727 (library
bound) | ISBN 9781538281710 (6 pack) | ISBN 9781538281734 (ebook)
Subjects: LCSH: Counting--Juvenile literature. | Extraterrestrial beings--
Juvenile literature.
Classification: LCC QA113.A68 2023 | DDC 513.2'11--dc23

Published in 2023 by
Gareth Stevens Publishing
29 East 21st Sreet
New York, NY 10010

© 2021 Booklife Publishing
This edition is published by arrangement with Booklife
Publishing

Edited by:
Emilie Dufresne

Illustrated by:
Amy Li

Printed in the United States of America

CPSIA compliance information: Batch #CSGS23: For further information contact Gareth Stevens,
New York, New York at 1-800-542-2595.

Find us on

Photo Credits

Images are courtesy of Shutterstock.com. With thanks to Getty Images,
Thinkstock Photo and IStockphoto.

Recurring images – Gwens Graphic Studio (stars and sparkles),
Vector Tradition (number pattern), RODINA OLENA (carpet pattern),
Tartila (electricity in generator). Cover – An1998, p1 – An1998,
p8 – Pretty Vectors, p10 – Pretty Vectors, p12 – Pretty Vectors,
Viktorija Reuta, p20 – Pretty Vectors, Viktorija Reuta, Spicy Truffel.

Nina likes to make aliens.

Her aliens do not always turn out as she planned.

This alien has

1 eye.

Nina tries again.

This alien has 2 eyes.

But they are on 2 heads!

Oh dear, Nina.

Try again!

The head is good!

But now there are 3 mouths.

3 mouths does not seem right.

Try again!

Now there are **4** mouths

and also **4** hands. No!

It is all going wrong!

Nina needs a new plan.

Now the alien has **5** noses!

Can you count them all?

Oh dear. Nina checks her plan.

Can you count how many legs there should be?

1 2 3 4 5 6

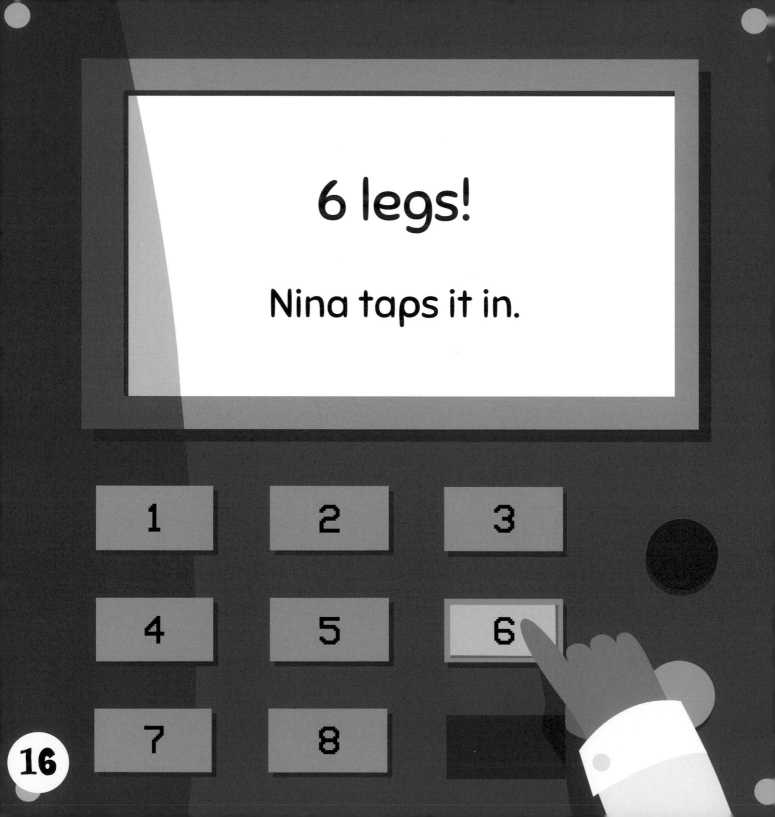

6 legs!

Nina taps it in.

6 legs – yes!

But **7** ears. Argh!

Oops. That is a lot of toes!

Can you count the toes?

1
2
3
4
5
6
7
8

This is not going well. What is wrong?

Boing!

20

A number is missing!

Can you count to the missing number?

1 2 3

4 5 6

7 8

Number 9 was missing all along.

Last try!

Well done, Nina!

This alien has

10

arms for hugging!

Can you count with aliens?

1 2 3 4

5 6 7 8

9 10